The Comedy Guide of Secrets to Making People Laugh

By
Butch Spillman

1

Introduction

If people have said, "You're such a Comedian", you probably are a natural comedian. But comedy can also be learned. This book is an easy to understand guide to help you excel in comedy.

Learn what makes people laugh, types of comedy routines, how to write jokes, how to do stand-up comedy, how to handle a heckler, how to market yourself like the best comedians, and so much more.

You won't find sugarcoated material that pumps you up, only to be let down later. Instead, you will be given realistic, tried-and-true information and practical advice, that will help you become a great comic.

This guide will groom you through every step you will face as you launch your career in live comedy.

If you can, would you please write an honest review? It only takes a minute. I would appreciate it and it really helps. Thanks...

Respectfully,
Butch Spillman

TABLE OF CONTENTS

Chapter One
What Makes People Laugh at Popular Comedians?

What is it that makes us laugh? Whether it be a light chuckle or that deep belly laugh that makes your sides hurt, there is something magical about laughter. It makes us feel better and lessens our burdens, even if we are laughing at our own shortcomings or weird phobias.

Laughter is contagious and this is why experts say we are fifty percent more likely to laugh when in social situations than when alone. This is why stand-up comedy brings in so many laughs. It is the crowd that makes the performance. Otherwise, it is just a person in front of a mic in a dark room, making jokes about their mom. Sounds creepy, right?

Laughter may start off with one or two people and then it quickly spreads to the entire room. Even if other people do not find the original cause of the laughter to be funny, they will end up laughing at a person who is genuinely having a big belly laugh.

Have you ever saw someone laughing, had no clue why they were laughing, but instantly began laughing yourself? Aunt Bertha is bent over in a fit of laughter and you can't help yourself from joining in because the sights and sounds of the laughter outbreak are just too appealing.

The science of laughter is not quite what you think

Many people believe the number one reason people laugh is because they hear a funny joke but this is not entirely so. People are more likely to laugh when they are interacting with others. This is why it is so important stand-up comedians engage their audiences and make them a part of the show.

According to scientists, there is no one formula that makes something funny. In other words, this book cannot show you a step-by-step, methodical way of being funny. However, it will point you in the right direction of discovering how to be funny in stand-up comedy.

Although scientists cannot offer a specific algorithm to make a stand-up show funny to an audience, they do give us some valuable insight. According to many years of research, scientists have discovered what truly makes us laugh is expecting one thing and then getting another. In a matter of seconds, what the brain was expecting is completely turned around. This is why the right punch line to a joke can send people into laughing hysterics.

Stand-up comedy shows need a bit of science and a whole lot of ingenuity to be a success. You will not be able to read this book and immediately jump on the new stand-up comedy stages and become one of the best comedians. You cannot expect to become a comedy great overnight so it is important you discover all you can about stand-up comedy so you can incorporate these truths into your routine and become better at telling jokes.

Are you really as funny as you think you are?

Laugh and the world laughs with you; tell a bad joke and you're on your own. Trying to discover what makes someone funny can be a bit difficult and even downright perplexing. You know you like stand-up comedian A because he makes you laugh but why does he make you laugh? Why is stand-up comedian B less funny?

Each of us gets our humor from the selective life experiences we have been through. Because humor is very much subjective, what one person finds funny won't even cause another to crack a grin. That is why the jokes that make the guys at the office laugh their butts off will fall on deaf ears at your spouse's family get-together.

Although your family and friends might think you are hilarious, chances are, they have experienced much of the same life experiences as you. This means their opinion is not very reliable at all. Sorry to burst your bubble!

Your mom might think you are hilarious but remember, she thinks it is still funny to tell your date about the time you ran around with your diaper on your head. Moms should never be the reason you label yourself as funny, or good-looking, for that matter.

So, is it possible to measure just how funny you are? Can you even begin to determine if you are actually funny enough to make it to the big stage? After all, it helps to have some skills in making people laugh if you want to do well in stand up comedy, right?

Check the subtle clues people exhibit when you are telling jokes

The true measure of knowing whether you are funny or not is being able to read people. It's not just their laughter that alerts you to your comedy prowess, it's about reading the subtle clues that let you know you can keep going with your jokes or you need to keep your day job. When you can master the art of reading people, you will know whether or not they truly find you funny.

When you begin telling jokes or funny stories with a group of friends, stop focusing so much on your delivery and start watching for subtle clues. After all, anyone can pretend to laugh but true laughter cannot be faked. People not only laugh with their mouths, they laugh with their entire bodies.

You will see their laughter in their eyes when they are truly laughing. They will lean in closer because they want to hear more. If you find people are distancing themselves from you during your joke-telling, it means they are feeling uncomfortable and you are not engaging your audience.

Do you find people subtly rolling their eyes when you start to tell a joke? Do they check their watch or phone several million times as you go on and on, delivering one punch line after another? If you are seeing these signs, chances are, you are not quite as funny as you think.

On the other hand, if people crowd around you to hear your funny stories at parties and you are able to retain their attention throughout your montage of jokes, you may have what it takes to engage an audience on the stand up comedy stage.

If you desperately want to be funny but find you aren't, all hope is not lost. There are actually proven methods you can use to make yourself come across as funny, even if you are not.

While these tips may not instantly make you the life of the party at all times, they will certainly help you to begin to develop a better sense of humor so you can pursue your dreams of becoming one of the top comedians.

How to be funny when you don't have a funny bone

So, what can you do when you truly want to be a standup comedian but your funny bone is seriously lacking or even non-existent? Is it ridiculous to think you can make yourself funny?

If you find it difficult to be funny, this area of the book will help you, even if you never make the final decision to pursue live comedy. Humor is important in life because it makes people feel more comfortable around you and makes you more interesting to others, whether you are writing a newsletter for your job or going on a first date with that special someone.

If you feel you do not have a natural sense of humor, you do not have to force it, but you also cannot sit back and expect it to happen without some work. Even if you are not particularly funny to others, you can make them laugh if you do one of these three things.

- Surprise your audience with something unexpected
- State the overly obvious
- Be subtle with your humor

One of the most important things to remember when you are trying to be funny is not to step completely outside of your comfort zone. If you lean on the conservative side, trying to suddenly tell explicit jokes to get a laugh is going to make you feel extremely uncomfortable.

Your audience is going to be able to pick up on your discomfort and your comedy will seem forced rather than natural. This will make you look like an awkward teen meeting your date's parents for the first time and it won't be pretty.

It is best to start with a form of humor that is most like who you are. If you are a quiet introvert, subtle humor is likely more your game. You may find it helpful to even make jokes about how shy you are. This is a great tool to use to make people laugh with you, instead of at you.

Do you know your audience?

One of the biggest mistakes unfunny people make when trying to be funny is not knowing their audience. You wouldn't want to share an explicit joke at church or be sarcastic with someone who is insecure. If you do not know your audience, the jokes you tell could fall on deaf ears or even backfire.

You need to make sure you can read your audiences before you try out jokes with friends or people you meet. Get to know people a bit before you branch out into trying to be funny. That way, you will not alienate your audience and make yourself look like a fool.

The following are some of the most important tips for making yourself funny. If you begin to purposely practice these, you will find yourself opening up to a whole new level of humor in your life, which will help you get that much closer to performing in a stand up comedy show.

- If you find yourself being too uptight, it is time to loosen up. Sometimes people that think they are not funny are simply taking life way too seriously. Make it a practice to smile and laugh as much as possible.

- It is important you are comfortable with yourself. If you are not comfortable with yourself, others are not going to be comfortable with you. People who have a natural sense of humor are generally able to laugh at themselves and at their own opinions. If you cannot joke about yourself, chances are, you won't be able to create jokes others will find funny.

- Learning to look for humor in everyday situations is one of the best ways to teach yourself to lean towards being funny. Many comedians find their material from the situations they face in life. If you truly practice this, you will begin to find humor in otherwise boring situations.

- Hanging out with funny people is also a big help. Surrounding yourself with funny people will help you to start to mimic some of their behaviors. As they say, if you surround yourself with funny people, their humor will start to rub off on you. Since your funny bone is lacking, you are going to need all the inspiration you can get.

- Because humor does not come naturally to you, you will need to practice. Although it might seem counterproductive to practice so you can become naturally funny, this is what you will have to do in the beginning. The more you can practice the art of comedy, the easier you will find it to be funny in social situations, in everyday life, and eventually on the comedy stage.

The important thing to remember when you are learning to be funny is to take your time and hone your skills. You are not going to become a great comedian overnight and it takes practiced skill to get up in front of an audience and be successful at getting laughs.

Now that you know a little more about how to launch into being funny, you will learn more about the stand-up comedy world and how you can break into it. To really appreciate stand-up and all it has to offer, you need to learn a bit about the history and the different types. This information will help you to begin to choose your path as a comedian so you can gather skills and confidence.

Chapter Two

Types of Stand-Up Comedy Shows

Famous comedians are not born, they are created. Although your friends and family might think you are the funniest person they have ever seen, this does not mean you are ready to hit the stage of a stand-up comedy club.

No one is born with an innate ability to make people laugh. This is a skill that is developed over time and through trial and error, although it does take a certain comedic personality to be able to develop humor people can appreciate.

In this chapter, you will learn a bit about the history of stand-up comedy and the different types famous comedians practice. You will also learn some hints that will help guide you into choosing the right type of stand-up comedy script to reflect your personality and help you win over the audience.

~A brief history of live comedy and the impact it has made on the world~

Unless you have been living under a rock, you have likely heard of many stand comedy greats in your lifetime. Although stand-up comedy is a true American art form, many people do not know where it originated or how it became such a presence in our world today.

People are often quite surprised to learn how top comedy shows first began in the United States. Believe it or not, Charles Dickenson once believed Americans to be a very unfunny group of people. Yes, it is shocking to hear that after we now have so many great comedians in our midst.

Although he certainly was not a stand-up comedian as we know them to be today, Mark Twain is believed to be one of the first to use humor as a primary subject in his speaking engagements held all over the country.

Twain is responsible for a term stand-up comedians still use today - bits. Comedians use the term "bits" for their jokes because they typically tell the most important points of a story to get a laugh or two. Twain was famous for telling his audiences he could not share the entire story but would give them the most important "bits."

Other fathers of stand comedy include the likes of Artemus Ward, who is often referred to as the first stand-up comedian. It is said this comedian was a favorite of President Abraham Lincoln. Another great in the earliest forms of stand-up comedy routines is Augustus Baldwin Longstreet who was one of the pioneer humorists. He was respected for being highly educated and funny.

As you delve a little farther into the history of stand-up komedi, you are sure to be brought to the 1930s and 40s, when stand-up comedy truly began to rise more into the form we know it as today.

As the best comedians began to rise, topics of humor ranged from "take my wife" to "my bossy mother." Comedians began to use their life experiences and turned them into monologues that spoke to the audience and helped them to feel at ease and escape for a bit into the world of humor and laughter.

What began as nightclub routines in dark and smoky bars later spilled over into television acts when television began to become popular in the late 1940s and 50s. Here, stand-up comedians were put before a much greater audience and stand-up comedy began to rise in popularity and controversy.

Today, stand-up show comedians are found in every race, gender, and a variety of ages. More and more women are now taking the reigns of new stand-up comedy shows and the playing field is ripe with opportunity for all types of comedians. If you have ever considered standing up before a crowd and delivering a comedy act, there is no better time in history to learn how to do stand-up comedy.

~Understanding the types of stand-up comedies~

You likely have favorite top comedians you like to listen to because of their style and the type of humor they deliver. Whether its the guy who always harps on his wife or the woman who likes to joke about her bad luck, there are tons of comedic styles out there to study.

The important goal of learning about the different types of stand-up comedy routines is to give you insight so you can find one you like and then hone your routine into one that truly reflects your personality and style.

You might think stand-up comedy simply involves a mic stand and the comedian but there is much more to getting a laugh from the audience. Developing a signature style is important for standing out amongst the many comedic greats who have gone before you.

Here are a few of the basic types of comedic performers you will experience when you travel the nightclub scene or watch comedians on comedy cable channels. Many stand-up comedians do not fit neatly into these categories because they excel at many types of stand-up comedy. When you can master more than one type, you will find you are able to appeal to a greater audience.

Impressionism – Have you ever heard a stand-up comedian that has the ability to do a perfect impression? They are so good at impersonating others, you could close your eyes and think you are hearing the person being impersonated. Do you find yourself making people laugh because you can perfectly impersonate your boss? Do you have a celebrity impression that is spot-on and always gets a good belly laugh? Impressionism is an integral part of stand-up comedy and is one of the most entertaining ways to branch out into the vast world of stand-up. If you want to study a great in impressionism comedy, check out Rich Little's routines and you will get a feel for how amazing impression skills can be.

Edgy – Edgy comics are the ones that tell it like it is. They are considered unfiltered and often controversial. A certain level of controversy is vital if you want to become well-known but how far is too far? Are you willing to go over the edge for the sake of comedy? Edgy comedians are both loved and hated and there is a fine line between both. They often say what everyone else is thinking but is too afraid to say. To study this type of stand-up comedy style, check out the likes of Lenny Bruce, George Carlin, and Bill Hicks. Being edgy doesn't mean you have to go as dark as some of these guys but studying their routines will give you some perspective on how deep edginess can run when it is unleashed on an audience.

Self-deprecation – Are you the type of person who makes others laugh at you because you make fun of yourself? Do you like being the butt of the joke? If you feel comfortable being the punch line, then self-deprecation humor is likely right up your alley. This type of comedian knows their problems and limitations and will point them out to you and make you laugh about them before you get a chance to put them down.

It's like the kid who makes fun of himself for being fat to keep from crying. Famous self-deprecators include Rodney Dangerfield, Joan Rivers, and Louis CK.

Deadpan – Like the name suggests, this form of stand-up comedy comedian is as dry as the toast your mom made you eat every morning before school. This act hinges on the comedian's ability to act emotionless, even when delivering the punch line of a joke. If you can keep a stone cold expression while delivering the best joke you ever heard, you might just be a deadpan comedian. With a monotone voice and a dead-behind-the-eyes stare, these comedians make people laugh by delivering hilarious material and never reacting to it as being funny themselves. The best deadpans in the history of comedy are Steven Wright, Mitch Hedberg, and Tig Notaro. Check out their routines to see if this type of comedy floats your boat.

Observational humor – This is one of the most common types of stand-up comedy working its way through the comedy clubs of America. This type of comedian sits back and observes life and then makes jokes out of it. The humor comes from their observations of commonplace life situations most people would not even think on, much less get a laugh from. This stand-up comedian typically relies on longer monologues regarding life stories they may or may not have actually experienced. To learn more about this style, study Eddie Murphy, Jerry Seinfeld, and Chris Rock.

Musical comedy – Musical comedy is a unique branch of stand-up comedy that brings humor from musical lyrics performed by the comedian. The vast majority of comedians that like this style do not use it for their entire stand-up routine. Instead, they sprinkle it in at just the right moments, to engage their audience and pull them back in. Musical comedy can help you stand out from the crowd and give your act an added spark that makes you unique. If you have a penchant for writing songs or playing instruments, you can incorporate these into your stand-up act and wow crowds. Some of the funniest musical comedians include Tom Lehrer, Steve Martin, and Adam Sandler.

Character comedy – Have you ever heard a comedian create a character and begin to voice this made-up person as if they exist? The comedian becomes the character they have made-up and they do it so well, their fans have a difficult time separating them from their character persona. When you become a character comedian, the character you develop can be entirely different from yourself. If you are shy, the character can be outgoing or the life of the party. Some comedians prefer this type of style because it allows them to act out fantasies of the type of personality they always wanted to have but couldn't in real life. If you are looking for character comedy role models, look no further than Andy Kaufman, Flip Wilson, or George Carlin, just to name a few.

Topical humor – Over the last few decades, topical comedians have grown in great numbers. If you don't believe it, just watch a few late night talk shows and you will get your fill. A topical comedian gets their material straight from the most recent news headlines. If you choose this style, your entire stand-up comedy routine needs to be full of pop culture references that speak to the issues of today and poke fun at them. This style of stand-up can also merge with other styles, depending on how a stand-up comic wants to deliver the goods. If you would like to study up on this type of comedy, be sure to watch Conan O'Brien, Dennis Miller, and Jon Stewart.

Improvisational – Improv comedy is one of the toughest types to master because there is no stand-up comedy script to go by. In fact, the comedian that steps to the improv stage does not in any way plan their act or rehearse. Instead, they are typically given a certain period of time to perform on stage and they must come up with material to get their audience laughing within seconds. If you are interested in learning how to be a stand-up comedian, learning improv is a fun way to start. Popular comedians that have mastered improv include Robin Williams, Paula Poundstone, and Wayne Brady.

Insult – When you consider some of the best comedy shows, there is always a bit of insult involved. Insult comedy comics hurl offensive insults at their audience. Not only do they get away with it, they actually get a laugh. If you have ever seen someone get "roasted," this is precisely the type of comedy you are witnessing. Insult comedians need to know how far they can go with an insult and what is too far. They must push to the point of crossing the line and then pull themselves back as needed, so they do not alienate their audience. Famous insulters include Don Rickles, Ricky Gervais, and Bob Saget.

Heritage – Heritage comedians like to poke fun at their own heritage and the stereotypes that are often associated with them. Heritage, sometimes referred to as cultural comedians, joke about their family traditions, religious practices, and stereotypes. Although this can sometimes be a risky type of comedy to pursue, it has allowed many comics to showcase their acts in new comedy shows all over the country. Some of the funniest heritage comics include Gabriel Iglesias, Chris Rock, and Richard Pryor. Study their comedy specials and you are sure to get the inspiration you need.

Although there are some other types of popular comedian routines, these are the most common types and for good reason. These types of routines get the audience engaged and make them burst out in laughter.

Studying the different types of comedy is vital for helping to ensure you are able to find the right one to speak to your particular sense of humor, or at least the one you would like to have.

How to find your comedic voice in stand-up comedy

One of the most difficult parts of finding your comedic voice is discovering which type of stand-up comedy appeals to you most. As we discussed earlier, finding the right style is important for ensuring you feel as comfortable as possible with the types of jokes you will be using when you hit the stage.

After you have watched all your favorite comics as much as possible and taken in some live shows, you should have a better idea of which style of stand-up most appeals to you.

What it boils down to, is experimentation. In the beginning, you are likely going to need to experiment with a variety of styles so you can choose one that gives you confidence and makes you shine on stage.

Experimenting with friends and taking advantage of open mic opportunities will allow you to try out your options and even fail a time or two. Failure should never be seen as actually failing at your craft. It is all about the processing of learning and realizing that some jokes or styles are just not going to work out for you and that's okay.

Do not think of a bad performance as a huge letdown. Instead, think of it as a learning experience and an opportunity to grow. All of the experience you get under your belt, whether good or bad, will help you to better become the performer you want to be.

What is a comedic voice?

Now that we have begun talking about finding your comedic voice, you may still be wondering exactly what this means. To better understand the importance of finding your comedic voice in stand-up, let's look to branding.

Think about how companies come up with products, whether it be a new type of cereal or a car. The company knows they have a lot of competition to go up against so they need to create their own unique style, taste, or service.

You too will have to create your own brand that helps you to stand out from the many stand-up comedians in the world. Remember, audiences like variety but you cannot meet all of the needs of every audience you stand before.

Instead of trying to be everything and failing at each style, it is best to choose your own unique style and stick with it. If you stick with what works for you and work it to the point of perfection, you are going to be able to thoroughly delight your audience. This is creating your own comedic voice. It is the style you will use to make yourself stand out from others so people will want to take the time to see your show or watch your video.

When thinking about finding your comedic voice, there are a few different questions you should ask yourself and take note of the answers.

- What is funny about you?
- Are there any stereotypes you fit into?
- Is there anything about your career that is funny?
- Is there anything funny about the town or country you come from?
- What is funny about your life and how you live it?
- What do you find funny?

Getting the answers to these questions will give you surprising insight into your potential style and even what you can begin to joke about on stage. Being able to truthfully answer these questions is the beginning of finding who you are as a comedian and what you would like to expound on in your journey towards hitting the big stage.

Chapter Three

What Does It Take to Perform Live Comedy?

While you might feel perfectly at ease "performing" jokes in front of your friends and family, getting up on the stage and performing live comedy is not so easy. Here, there is no forgiving audience and people will let you know very quickly if they are not happy with what you are saying.

This is not to dissuade you from pursuing your dreams but you do need to be aware of what you face when you start out in stand-up. The more realistically prepared you are, the better!

One of the first things we need to discuss regarding live stand-up comedy performances is making sure you have the guts. As they say, without the guts, you will never get the glory.

Do you have the guts for stand-up comedy shows?

One of the biggest obstacles people face when pursuing a career in stand-up comedy is fear. Fear often keeps people from being able to pursue their dreams.

Fear can actually cripple a person if they allow it to take over.

Overcoming fear and gaining courage is vital for having the guts you need to get up on stage. If you are shy and timid, you may find it difficult at first. You are not going to suddenly begin feeling comfortable on stage right away. It might take a little time but with time and effort, things will get easier.

When you are working on overcoming your fears, it is helpful if you first list all of the fears you have about getting on stage. What is the worst that could happen? When considering your fears about getting on stage, you need to have the ability to separate the true worries and those that are not anything to be concerned about.

If you can separate true concerns over unfounded ones, you will be able to better deal with your fears and overcome them. When you can face your fears, you will realize none of them is a life and death concern.

Although your audience might boo or heckle you, that is the worst that could happen. You might be embarrassed but an audience can only do so much to you. Even if your first performance or two does not go all that well, you should not take it as a failure. Use it to learn from your mistakes and better your performance so your next stand-up routine will be stellar.

One of the most important things you can do to prepare yourself for stand-up comedy is to reduce your fear as much as possible and increase your confidence. In the beginning, you may have to fake confidence but the more you step to that stage and perform your routine, the better the chances of you gaining the confidence you need.

Most audiences are going to want to see you succeed so they can get their money's worth out of your performance. If you do find a particular audience is less than welcoming, chalk it up to a learning experience and move on. It is just that simple.

How to polish your stage presence

Stage presence is another important element of being able to make it as a stand-up comedian. Stage presence can make or break your performance so you need to make sure you polish your stage presence as much as possible.

Although stage presence can come naturally for some, it certainly does not for everyone. Many of your favorite comedians likely struggled when they first started out. No comedian you ever meet will be able to truthfully tell you there were no bumps along the way.

Thankfully, having the right stage presence is something that can be taught and this section of the book will offer you tips and insight into making sure you are prepared. Like with any part of the process of becoming a stand-up comic, the more you practice, the better you will become as you stand up before audience after audience and perfect your routine.

There are a few different elements to making sure your stage presence is where it should be.

- You must remember when you become a stand-up comedian, the show is all about your audience and not about you. Your audience is there to be entertained and it is your job to make sure they enjoy the show. You cannot successfully accomplish this if your focus is not on putting the audience first.
- Your audience needs to feel safe and they can only do this if you are confident. If you get up on stage and cannot hold your composure, your audience is going to feel uncomfortable and they will not feel safe enough to allow you to entertain them and

make them laugh. Remember, they are there to see you excel, not squirm on stage.

- As we said above, your performance is all about your audience and you need to give them what they want. A professional stand-up comedian knows their audience and they are confident they can deliver exactly what their audience is wanting.
- Although it may work for you to take baby steps in the beginning, most people discover taking big chances and diving off the cliff of their comfort zone makes it easier to progress in their ability to entertain audiences.

Perfecting your personality on stage

The personality you choose to have on stage is crucial for your stand-up act. The personality you choose may be very much different from your own. The wonderful thing about stand-up is, you can create any type of personality you like, as long as it is one that entertains your audience.

You may find yourself creating multiple personalities or sticking to one, depending on how you want to perfect your act. Neither way is wrong so you will need to decide which option works best for you.

Some comics like using different stage personalities because this allows them to keep their routine fresh and gives them the option of customizing their performance to match the audience they are standing before.

Effective and entertaining comedians realize honing their on-stage personality takes time. Perfection will not happen overnight or even within a few weeks. Some comedians take months and even years to fully perfect their on-stage persona so do not feel you have to rush the process.

Just remember, they do not call it an "act" for nothing. You will basically need to act on stage, creating a character to portray and a dialogue to entertain with. Unless you are performing improvisational comedy, your act will need to be rehearsed and ready when you go on stage. As you learn to polish your persona and performance, you will find your act becomes easier to pull off and you will be able to make it look as if it was never rehearsed.

These are the most important components of becoming a stand-up comedian that truly gets the right response from their audience. Although at first, it can seem a bit overwhelming, you can make it happen if you are willing to give it your all and keep trying, no matter how many times you might fall.

Chapter Four
How to Write Stand-Up Comedy Jokes

One of the most difficult tasks to accomplish on your road towards becoming a stand-up comedian is writing your material. You may find yourself "quick-witted" when it comes to laughing around with your friends but find it nearly impossible to sit down and think about writing jokes on paper.

Your natural sense of humor is what you display when you are able to offer funny quips with your friends. The problem is, aspiring stand-up comedians attempt to write comedy from a very strategic standpoint.

Instead of reacting naturally to a situation and writing something funny about it, they "force" their comedy writing by attempting to write a joke or reaction they *think* a stand-up comedian should have. This never works!

Use every day experiences to create hilarious jokes and stories

If you have ever sat around with a group of friends and retold funny stories that have happened, you already know the basic premise of writing stand-up material. Life is full of downright hilarious moments, even when the moment is only funny later.

Stand-up comedy experts recommend people take a small notepad and pen with them everywhere they go. You just never know when inspiration for new material might strike. Keeping a notepad and jotting down funny ideas throughout the day will give you a reference point for writing material.

People like to hear stories and jokes about real life, even if you have to embellish them a little. Truly funny stories and jokes often come from real experiences a comic has had in life.

Think about all the funny stories that have been passed down in your family. As you are working your day job or going about your life, you are bound to see and experience things that make you laugh.

Chances are if they make you laugh, they are going to make others laugh too. You just need to make sure you are able to re-tell the story so your audience gets a full picture of what is occurring and can see it all take place in their mind. If you are vivid enough in the details of your recollection, you will have a much better chance of getting a laugh from your audience.

When you are using real-life experiences to create your jokes for stand-up comedy shows, you will need to be able to properly share the context of the situation and what made it so funny. The punch line will only make sense if you are able to fully set up the scene in the minds of your audience so they can truly understand the context of what you are trying to share with them.

Once you start looking at life as one big comedy stage, you will realize you are constantly being bombarded with new material for your act. You will then need to take this inspiration, remove some of the fluff that makes your joke or story boring, and then add in details that further bring the funniness home to your audience.

Mastering the art of setup and punch line

Before you begin writing your own material, you need to know the important parts of joke-telling. Many new comedians have a hard time being able to recognize all of the important components of a joke because they have never sat down with a comedian and realized all the work that is involved in creating what seems to the audience to be a simple joke.

One of the most common forms of joke-telling on comedy stages across the country is the setup and punch line delivery. This is a joke form that many new comedians rely on to help them keep a simple formula for making sure they get a laugh from their audience.

A basic setup and punch line joke consists of three important parts. These parts all work together to surprise the audience into laughing. Understanding how each of the joke parts works and why it is important will allow you to more easily construct your jokes so they flow more naturally.

The Premise – Comedians like Louis CK seem like masters at joke-telling because they know how to set up the premise properly. If you do not set up the premise of your joke, you are going to end up leaving your audience confused because they will not "get" your punch line. The premise of the joke is the reason someone should find it funny. The premise can be good or bad and you will set up the mood of the premise by the tone of your voice. If your premise is clear enough, you will be able to setup your punch line.

The Setup – Some comedians consider this the most significant of the three parts, and perhaps, they are correct. Without the setup, the premise will be misunderstood and the punch line will not be deliverable. The setup provides a succinct example of the premise. You want to get the point of your joke across in as few words as possible. If your setup is too long, your audience will likely forget the premise of the joke and then the punch line, when delivered, will no longer make sense to them. You will need to continue working your setup and whittling it down until it fully supports your premise but does so without too much fluff and banter.

The Punch Line – Now, we come to the single most important part of the joke you are telling – the Punch Line. Without a punch line, a joke is not a joke. Although the punch line is of extreme importance, it does not stand alone. If you were to hit the stage with only punch lines, your audience would think you had gone mad. The punch line is the twist to the story. Your audience is expecting one thing, but you deliver another. As we talked about earlier in the book, this is what makes people laugh. You need to be good at finding the surprise in every joke-telling experience or your audience is not going to find you funny.

Once you have delivered your punch line, it is time to stop talking immediately. You wait for your laugh and pray you get it! If you continue talking after the punch line, you will break into the laugh of your audience because they will naturally stop laughing so they can hear what you are saying. The punch line needs to be delivered as if you just threw the best hand on the card table. Deliver it with confidence and then stand back and watch as they laugh.

This kind of joke delivery allows for a natural ebb and flow during stand-up comedy shows. You will need to know when to speak and when to let your audience roll with laughter. At all times, you need to be in charge of the stage but you also need to let your audience in on the performance because, without their laughter, it would be nothing.

Okay, so let's put this together and see how it works out on the stage. If you follow these steps, you will be able to master setups and punch lines so you can feel confident performing at any stand-up show.

Step One – You will need to state your premise, making sure you use the right tone of voice for how you want the audience to perceive your premise, whether it be good or bad.

Step Two – You will then need to set up your premise by telling the audience the example, incident, or observation that sets up your premise. Again, make sure the tone of your voice is unmistakable in helping your audience to fully understand the premise of the joke you are attempting to convey. If you do this step correctly, you will have no trouble delivering your punch line.

Step Three – Now, it is time to deliver your punch line and you need to make it a zinger. The punch line needs to be the exact opposite of what your audience is expecting. You will have a certain tone throughout your joke and then you will change your tone to deliver your punch line in a shocking way. The right delivery is the key to success in joke-telling. Practice, practice, practice the delivery of your punch line and make sure you get it right. Your comedy performance depends on it!

Use this formula for writing your stand-up comedy script jokes with ease

Writing jokes will, at first, seem overly complicated. This is because you are new to writing jokes and you want to make the best first impression you possibly can on stage. The formula I am about to share with you is used by some of the best stand-up comedians all over the world. The formula is easy to use and will help you start off on the right foot in your stand-up comedy pursuit so you can begin to get some jokes down on paper and start rehearsing.

Step One- You will need to create a premise and it doesn't have to be funny. It could be anything really. For instance, you could say, "I hate turnips." Write down your premise and then move on to step two.

Step Two – Next, you just need to sit down and really think about the statement you just made. Why is it true? What are some facts that support the statement you just made? At this point, you do not care about being funny. You are simply trying to brainstorm and write down as many facts about your premise as possible. You can get as crazy as you like in this step so just let your brain do its thing and jot down everything you come up with, even if it seems boring or even silly.

Step Three – Now, it is time to shuffle through all the facts and information you just put down on paper. You need to look through these to determine which ones really stand out. Which are unique? Which statements are interesting? Choose the ones that are the best – the ones that really catch your eye and make you think. This step is going to end up producing your punch line. Pair your premise with one of the facts or pieces of information you wrote down. You will then need to share your new jokes with friends and family and get their input until you find one that works.

The point of having a joke formula in place is just to get you thinking about consistency. Your joke can be about anything and you can make people laugh if you know your audience, choose wisely and deliver properly.

You are not going to be able to start off being perfect so do not even strive for it. In the beginning, your jokes may lack something that makes them funny so you will need to keep working this formula and keep trying new subjects.

Look around you for inspiration and don't let your mind get bogged down with the details. As you learn to use the formula to your advantage, you will find yourself being able to master joke writing so you can use this formula to observe and gain material for jokes.

Chapter Five
How to Perfect Your Stand-Up Comedy Routine

You now know what it takes to be a stand-up comedian and how to begin writing some of your own material. Now that you have delved into the basics of stand-up, it is time to begin to hone your performance into something great.

Polishing your act is going to take time and dedication. You are reading this book because you are interested in launching into a stand-up comedy career and that is a vigorous first step.

Perfecting your stand-up routine is going to take some elbow grease and determination. You are not going to be able to accomplish it in twenty-four hours or even in a few days.

This chapter will help you realize the steps you can take to make sure your act is where it should be when you finally get the opportunity to go on stage. The more work you put into polishing your act, the better the chances of you and your audience having a great time as you throw jokes out to them. So, let's start to launch into the deep end of the pool. Put on your floaties if you are a little scared!

Practice in front of the mirror to get a feel for how you will be perceived

When it comes to practicing in front of a mirror, you are going to get varying opinions from stand-up comedians. Some swear by it and others refuse it. Working in front of a mirror can be advantageous because it can reveal how you will look to the audience as you perform.

Unfortunately, practicing in front of the mirror can also lead to over-acting because a person tries too hard to make the right facial expressions and gestures. This is why it is recommended mirror practice is not used as the sole means of perfecting your routine.

It should be used as one of a few different ways to capitalize on your humor and better perform before your audience. Mirror practice is especially important for the following components of certain types of stand-up routines.

- If you plan on doing a celebrity impression in your routine, being able to make the right faces and gestures is vital. Seeing yourself performing the impression in front of the mirror will help you to realize any areas that need work. This will help you see what your audience sees so you can perfect your impression.
- When planning to incorporate a character that is completely different from you, it is wise for you to consider practicing stand-up in front of a mirror. Practicing this character in front of a mirror will help you to better understand how the character will be perceived by your audience. This is a great way to refine your character presentation before you actually present it to a live audience.
- Some comedians incorporate magic tricks and props into their routine. If you plan on using props or magic tricks, performing in front of the mirror is almost a necessity. The mirror tells no lies and if you look like a moron playing with props in front of the mirror, you are going to look like a moron playing with props in front of your audience.

Allow the mirror to be your sounding board in helping you decide what you need to work on with your routine.

It is much easier to mess up in front of the mirror and not die of embarrassment than it is to get on stage and totally bomb. Work out the kinks in your routine while you are in front of the mirror and get things right before you continue.

Make your friends and family guinea pigs

Your friends and family should be your biggest supporters when it comes to launching your career in stand-up. If they aren't, then maybe you need to consider getting new ones!

True friends and family should be more than willing to allow you to try out your jokes to see if they work. When you have been practicing in front of the mirror, it is time to perform in front of friends. The best way to do this is to make it a fun time.

It is wise to treat this as an audition of sorts. Why not invite your friends and family over and make it a night of comedy? You could make an impromptu stage with a mic stand and perform your routine in front of your audience.

Ask them for their honest opinions and be ready to take notes on their criticism. Do not allow their reactions to dissuade you from pursuing your love of stand-up. Instead of getting embarrassed or even angry about their opinions, sit down and take time to think about them and see whether or not they are true. If you find them to be true, work on your act and keep trying.

It's time to shine on open mic nights

When you are just starting out in stand-up comedy, open mic opportunities will need to be sought as often as possible. If you are not familiar with open mic, (sometimes referred to as open mike) this is simply an event that is held in comedy clubs, music clubs, and other venues.

Open mic opportunities allow you to try out your routine without being as nervous as you would at a paid gig. Before scheduling your spot with an open mic event, you need to make sure you understand some of the rules of the road, so to speak.

The steps you take before, during, and after an open mic event could help further your opportunities in stand-up comedy or bring them crashing to the ground.

Since you are reading this book, you have likely never participated in an open mic, even so, let's first go over some do's and don'ts of the trade.

Do NOT expect to attend an open mic night and immediately be discovered. It rarely happens that way. An open mic night is an opportunity to network so you will need to do some work to follow up.

DO spend time getting to know everyone involved in the open mic night. Make sure to write down names and contact information so you can network with others who are doing the same thing as you.

Do NOT get up and perform and then leave the club when your time is up. This is one of the rudest things you can possibly do in an open mic opportunity and it will backfire on you. If you are not willing to watch the other performers, then do not bother coming! Open mic nights work because everyone gives feedback and tries to help each other. Don't be one of those jerks that abuses open mic night without doing their part.

DO make sure you do your best, even if you only have an audience of one. If you look out at the crowd and no one is paying attention, pretend they are. Open mics are about gaining experience and simply getting up on the stage and talking behind the mic is a big first step so don't blow it, no matter how small the audience might be.

Do NOT do any heckling at an open mic event, even if others are doing so. Think of yourself as being the one on stage and how you would feel if you were being heckled by some jerk in the audience. While open mics are meant to expose amateurs to the live comedy stage, heckling is generally considered classless, especially when its done by one of the fellow performers.

Do NOT talk loudly while someone else is performing. Although it is fine to have conversations, make sure you are being polite and not overshadowing a fellow performer's attempts to be on stage. The person who is on stage at the moment has the right to be seen and heard, not you!

Do NOT get up on stage and first start apologizing for how your comedy routine sucks. This immediately sets up your audience to expect failure and they will not have any level of excitement about your performance. Even if you think your performance is going to suck, do not let anyone else believe it.

DO make sure you have fun! Fun is what open mic night is all about, no matter the venue. If you are not having fun during these opportunities, chances are, you are not going to enjoy a career in stand-up comedy. Open mic nights are the most forgiving of any audience so enjoy yourself and help others to do the same.

Do NOT give generic criticism of other performers. If you truly want valuable insight into your own routine, make sure you give this to other performers as well. As you are watching other performers, take note of their name and what you liked best and least about their performance. Be as specific as possible without being mean or overly critical. Make sure you give a positive with every negative.

If you follow these do's and don'ts of proper etiquette, you will have a good time, meet helpful network contacts, and gain valuable insight into your stand-up comedy show performance.

Although you will be nervous even thinking about getting up on stage, do not let them see you sweat. This is a time for you to begin to fully see how your comedy act is welcomed by a live audience.

No matter the outcome, allow it to be a learning experience. Each time you take advantage of these open mic nights, you will gain confidence and skill. You will also meet people you can network with and who will help encourage you to keep going.

How to keep your stand-up material fresh and exciting

Another important thing you will need to do to perfect your stand-up comedy show is to make sure your act features the latest comedy. Comedy routines, just like any form of entertainment can become stale, especially when you have performed them often. Even if your act is making people laugh, that does not mean it is time for you to hang up your writing hat.

Always, always, always be on the lookout for new material. As we said before, make sure to keep a notebook and pen with you at all times and use them. Do not be afraid to try new things. If a new joke bombs, it might just be the wrong audience or time.

NEVER be afraid to fail! Some of the most brilliant comedians of our time failed miserably in their first attempts at becoming stand-up comics. If you do not let your routine evolve as you gain experience, you will never be successful.

Chapter Six
How to Market Yourself like the Best Comedians

Times have changed in the world of stand-up comedy and many believe the changes are for the better. With the Internet and many social media outlets, potential comedians now have more options than ever before for marketing themselves.

If you are a stand-up comedian in the twenty-first century, networking is your friend. You will need to put yourself out there so you can be noticed. We will talk about hiring a manager later in the book, but for now, we will focus on helping you manage your own career.

Marketing tips to help you get noticed

Because there is a great deal of competition in the stand-up world, you need to become your biggest fan and begin to market your comedy skills as much as possible. If you have not already, you need to make sure you open accounts on every social media platform available. Some of the top choices include:

- YouTube
- Facebook
- Twitter
- Instagram
- Reddit
- Vine
- Tumblr
- Pinterest
- Flickr

No matter the reason a person is attempting to market themselves on social media, it is imperative to be able to relate to and engage the audience. One of the biggest mistakes comedians make is simply using these social media platforms to showcase their talent and try to get a gig.

The problem with that method is the comedian never takes the time to get to know their followers and develop a relationship. There is no trust or care between the comedian and their followers so no relationship is forged.

If you want to truly use social media as a way to market yourself without being ostracized, you need to make sure you first and foremost make your accounts about your followers.

Engage their interest and make them feel as if they are a part of your career. This will make you matter to them and help you to grow in popularity because your followers will want you to succeed. This is one of the best first steps you can take in marketing your comedy skills.

Create your Electronic Press Kit

An Electronic Press Kit (EKO) is your professional comedian resume. It tells promotors, venue talent buyers, members of the press, talent managers, and other like-minded professionals why they should consider hiring you, writing about you, or seeking to partner with you.

In today's electronic age, it is not sufficient enough to only have social media accounts. Although these are important, they will not sell you as a comedian. The EPK is what provides the press with the information they need to write about you.

It is one of the easiest ways for you to be able to showcase your talent and get people interested in your work. If you do not have an Electronic Press Kit, your credibility as a professional performer is going to be questioned.

The basics of your EPK need to include the following.

- Your bio should be prominent in your EPK and should be both engaging and informative. It is important you create a nice balance between giving the facts and being entertaining at the same time. After all, if the information is incredibly boring, no one is going to want to read it.
- Examples of the work you do should also be featured. Videos are a great way to share your talent with the world. They should be featured on YouTube or Vimeo and should be embedded. If you post live videos, and you should, make sure they are clear and showcase your best work.
- You should include links to your social media pages so those who are interested can learn more about your work and who you are. This can often help to increase your followers on social media sites.
- Your contact info should be clearly displayed so it can be easily found. You may just be surprised

who begins to contact you for work when you have a truly polished and appealing EPK.

In the past, physical press kits were printed up and handed out by inspiring comedians but with the Internet, most professionals who are interested in your work are going to prefer an electronic method of learning about you.

If you are having difficulty creating your EPK, you may want to consider having a professional web designer help you create one. These services will cost you a little money but having that professional EPK in place can help open doors for you in your career.

How to develop your fan base

People are the most important thing when it comes to building your career. Building a relationship with people who like your comedy is paramount. Although it might seem a little overwhelming at first, it is fairly easy to begin growing your fan base if you will remain dedicated.

Blogs and websites –

The first step you will need to take is to find about five websites that feature blogs or forums where people talk about your same style of comedy. Once you have found these sites, start hanging out and regularly commenting. Get to know the people who frequent the site.

As you get to know people on these sites, you will eventually be given the opportunity to be able to share information on the work you do as a comedian. Because you have chosen the sites you interact with carefully, those you meet on these sites are likely to enjoy the same type of comedy you offer so they will be interested in your work.

YouTube –

New comedians need to take advantage of sites like YouTube which can dramatically help increase their fan base. Not only do you need to create your own channel and regularly post new videos, you also need to get to know the community.

Take time watching comedy videos that relate to your style of comedy. Check out the comments and begin interacting with those who comment. Make sure the comments and replies you leave on videos are clever with a tinge of funny.

Each time you comment, others will be able to see who you are and click through to your channel so they can subscribe or just begin watching your videos. This alone can substantially increase your fan base rather quickly.

Purchase Ads –

If you are willing to shell out a little money, purchasing Facebook ads can be lucrative for helping to increase your followers and spread the word about your comedy. Your Facebook ads can be targeted to people in the areas you perform comedy in. You can even target the ads to a specific age group or gender.

Many new comedians find purchasing Facebook ads to be well worth the expense they must pay out. You can always try it out and if it does not seem to bring in any followers or attention, you can focus your attention on other options that will bring in more volumes of people.

How to get hired for stand-up comedy show gigs

Once you have begun to develop a fan base and are feeling confident about your material, it is time to step into the limelight and start to get paying work. Before you launch out into the deep, it is important you are truly prepared for a gig. If you are not ready to provide at least 30 minutes of captivatingly funny material, then you are likely not yet ready to begin booking gigs.

One of the first things you need to consider is making sure you are ready to start at the bottom. If you have never headlined at a comedy club, you cannot immediately expect to start off headlining. One of the first gigs you are likely to be offered is an opener.

The opener comes out first and warms up the crowd. Depending on the club rules, this will likely only give you around five minutes of stage time. It is imperative you are able to give your very best for those five minutes so you can be remembered.

When you become the middle act, you may be on stage for as long as ten to fifteen minutes. When you become a headliner, you could be on stage as long as an hour, depending on the comedy club you are headlining at.

Do not think of yourself as being too good to take the lowly gig of being an opener. The job of opener may not seem as good as a headliner but you have to remember you are working towards a goal.

Although five minutes isn't long, it is long enough to make a lasting impression on the audience. Make sure you do your best and be consistent in getting laughs and you are sure to work your way up to becoming a headliner.

Contests might seem like a strange way to launch your career, but they can work. Believe it or not, show promoters often attend these stand-up comedy events so they can find up-and-coming talent. Even if you are not the winner of the contest, you can attract the attention of a promoter and end up getting booked for a gig.

It also never hurts to get to know headliners and ask them to be a part of their show. This especially works if you have worked with the headliners before during open mic events or as an opener for their headline event.

The more you get your name out there and the more you stand before audiences, no matter the role, the better the chances of you impressing promoters by making people roar with laughter.

It is in no way going to start off being easy but the more you work your game and perfect your act, the more attention you are going to garner from people who can help you progress in your career.

Chapter Seven
How to Do Stand-Up Comedy

It's one thing to know how to perform before your friends and family or how to get a few laughs at a party but it is an entirely different thing when you stand before a live audience. It is then when the nerves begin to kick in and you really begin to feel what being on the big stage is all about.

This chapter is going to help you with your stage presence and how to overcome the obstacles that will try to prevent you from feeling comfortable while standing before an audience.

It is time to learn how to dress and act the part so you can shine on stage and overcome those nerves and the disappointments that will inevitably come along the way.

How should you dress for stand-up comedy shows?

It is time to discuss the difficult subject of what should you wear on the stand-up comedy stage. Is there a dress code to adhere to? Is there a certain style comedians should wear to make a statement?

If you've ever seen any stand-up comedy acts, you know the types of clothing comedians wear on stage can range from downright bizarre to plain and mundane. Some comedians get the first laugh from their outfit alone.

What you wear on stage gives the audience the first clue of who you are. Often, they will form an opinion about you before you even open your mouth. So, should you dress to the nines or does pretty much anything go?

The answer to this question cannot be given in one single sentence because the "dress code" for comedians is more complicated than that. The best advice you can be given is to dress in something that makes you feel comfortable without making you look sloppy and unkempt.

Many people wear jeans and a T-shirt on stage because they are comfortable in these clothes. Wearing casual clothes helps you to not only feel comfortable but they also help the audience to focus on the jokes you are telling instead of on what you are wearing.

Wearing a flamboyant outfit with ten pockets, rhinestones, and gold is only going to draw attention to what you are wearing. Your entire routine will be missed because people will only be staring at your outlandish outfit.

Now, being casual does not mean wearing a pair of torn jeans and a stained shirt. Dress as if you are preparing for a casual date, without going overboard. This is not the time to show skin and you certainly should never plan on wearing shorts.

You may think that last statement sounds weird but there are many comedy clubs that will not even let you take the stage if you are wearing shorts. There have even been books written about this topic.

The point of your wardrobe is to make you feel confident without drawing attention to your outfit. Try on different looks and have someone take a full body shot of you so you can see what you look like from the audience's point of view.

Just remember to make sure your outfit is appropriate for an audience who will be seated below the level of the stage you are standing on. No short dresses, shorts, or other such attire should be worn because this can give the audience a show they were not expecting and could lead to embarrassment.

How to overcome the nerves

It's time for your very first gig and you are sweating bullets. Your skin is clammy and your heart is absolutely racing a mile a minute. Although you know it sounds silly, you feel like you are about to die.

Nervousness can truly attack your entire body and make you feel ill. If you've ever stood before a class and said a speech or been stopped by a police car, you know what it feels like.

What can you do when you feel anything but calm? How can you possibly overcome your nervousness and be able to calmly stand before a large audience and make them laugh?

Although time and experience help with overcoming nervousness, these tips can assist you in the beginning, when anxiety seems to rear its ugly head more than ever before.

Whether you call it nervousness, stage fright, or outright fear, getting up on stage in front of a bunch of people can be scary. It is especially frightening to know you are there to make them laugh and all eyes are on you. Allow the following tips to help calm you so you will be able to overcome your rattled nerves and find peace on stage.

- Deep breathing exercises might seem a bit silly to do but they actually work. When you focus on deep breathing, this slows down your heart rate and reduces your adrenaline production. It helps to envision yourself performing and being a success as you practice relaxing with deep breathing.
- It might be tempting to try and enhance your personality by drinking a shot of alcohol or guzzling an energy drink but this is not recommended. Drinking these beverages can end up making you jittery and increase your heart rate which is likely already elevated. Instead, drink plenty of water and eat a light meal, avoiding any spicy foods.
- Being in front of an audience of strangers can be extremely stressful. For the first few times, it will help to have a friend or two scattered in the

audience so you can look to them when you are feeling overwhelmed with fear and anxiety.

- If you feel really nervous up on stage, try to joke about it instead of letting it control you. This will help you get a laugh or two under your belt and make you feel more at ease during your performance.

- Distancing yourself from others just before you hit the stage can be very helpful for overcoming nervous jitters and channeling your energy into giving your best performance ever. Some of the top stand-up comedians recommend shutting off the radio, television, and phone. Get in a quiet place and think solely on your performance.

- It might seem silly but a pep talk can really help you overcome the nerves and psych you up so you are ready to kill it on stage. Stand in front of a mirror and give yourself a glowing pep talk, showcasing your abilities, your charm, and your ability to make others laugh. Even if you have to sneak away to the bathroom to do it, it will be worth it.

How to avoid getting overly discouraged in your stand-up career

Getting discouraged while you are attempting to rise in your stand-up career can be detrimental to your aspirations. The more discouraged you get, the less you will seek gigs and the more your career will begin to falter.

Discouragement is bound to come when you are first starting out in stand-up comedy shows. There are going to be failures and you are going to be turned down for gigs. This is just a big part of the stand-up comedy world and you are going to have to learn not to take it personally.

One of the biggest obstacles stand-up comedians face when they are trying to get over being discouraged is themselves. All too often, we constantly put ourselves down.

"You aren't good enough!"
"You aren't funny enough!"
"You are too boring!"
"You will never make it in stand-up comedy!"
"People don't like you!"

On and on, we fill our minds with this nonsense and then the scary thing is, we actually start to believe it. It is time you stopped listening to yourself and started talking to yourself instead.

You need to start feeding your mind positives so you can overcome the negatives that are trying to choke out your dreams. Even if you feel like the biggest loser on the planet because all your jokes fell on deaf ears and no one laughed, you need to tell yourself you are great.

Do not set yourself up for failure by speaking so many negatives into your life. When you exchange the positives for the negatives, you will be amazed at how much easier it is to stand on stage with confidence and not sweat the small stuff.

Another valuable hint that can help you avoid getting discouraged is to celebrate often. Instead of waiting to celebrate until you get your first big break, make sure you celebrate every positive moment along the way.

When you are constantly looking for things to celebrate in your stand-up comedy career, you will have no time for those nagging doubts to surface and you will be able to stifle those voices in your mind that try to tell you that you can't do it.

It's not rocket science, but these tips have been used by some of the best comedians in the world and they do work. The key to overcoming discouragement and negativity is to never let it have a voice in your life.

If you truly screwed up in a performance, learn from it and fix your mistakes. Don't dwell on it and move on! This is how you will get over those hurdles that seem to always rise up and stand in the way of you moving forward towards your dreams. These tips can honestly apply to anything in your life that may be causing you to become discouraged.

Chapter Eight
The Best Comedy Show Performance Tips

If you want to become one of the best comedians, you need to know how to make a big splash on the stage instead of doing an embarrassing belly flop. In this chapter, we will discuss important tips like getting the audience to pay attention and overcoming hecklers that might try to catch you off guard. This chapter is focused on helping you stay in control the entire time you are on stage, no matter how long your set is.

How to get the audience to listen to your stand-up show

If your audience is not paying attention to you, you will never get a laugh -it's just that simple. It is inevitable, you will stand before an audience at some point and find they are not paying any attention to you at all.

How can you possibly deliver the best stand-up comedy jokes when your audience is looking at their phones, talking amongst themselves, or even falling asleep? With these tips, even the coldest and most unresponsive audiences can be turned around. These trade secrets will help you rise above a challenging audience and win them over.

Even if your audience is stone cold, you will likely be able to find one or two people that are actually paying attention, even if they look bored to death. Instead of plowing straight through the material you planned, why not use this as an opportunity to practice playing up to the audience.

If you can get even a couple of people engaged in your act and laughing, you may be able to pull the rest of the audience in. Playful banter with the audience can be tough to master but this is a great way to practice.

Here are some additional tips to help you engage an audience who is not even aware of you being on stage, much less what you are saying.

- If you know an audience is a cold one, hit the stage and say something absolutely bizarre. This sounds really strange but it works at getting their attention. Do not say anything mean or offensive or this will end up backfiring on you. Step to the stage with confidence and say it so everyone's ears are pricked. Once you have their attention, make sure you use your best material in a conversational voice.

- Since you only have about thirty seconds to get their attention, start off with a funny self-deprecating joke and the crowd will likely grow more comfortable and actually listen to what you are about to say. Some of them will relate to the struggle you just talked about, whether it be your appearance, dating, or your job.

- When you step to the stage, your goal is to get your audience to applaud as a collective at least three times. If you do this, it will unify your audience and get them on your side. Try asking easy questions like, "Are you guys ready for an awesome show?" "Who here is tired of work?" or "Who wants to laugh?" You will be surprised what a little clapping can do for the energy of your audience.

- If you find your audience is less than attentive, do what top comedians do and change your voice. Sounds silly? Doing an odd-sounding impersonation or just changing the tone of your voice can wake up a sleepy audience and help you to gain their attention, even if you have not been able to get it before.

- While it might seem overly simple, moving around on stage can get their attention. If you feel like their eyes are glazing over and they are no longer listening, move from in front of the mic stand and walk to one side or the other of the stage. Moving a bit will get their attention and help to restore their focus on you and what you are saying.
- If the set is getting weak and your audience is getting bored, try acting out a funny story. Be the characters and mimic some of their movements. Audiences love funny stories, especially when they can relate to the story. You acting out the voices and movements will help them to feel as if they were there and they will respond better to your material.

How to get the audience to like you

A big part of getting the audience to like you is being relatable. People like others because they are able to see something in that person that they can relate to. This section offers tips on how to make the audience fall in love with you so you will get all the laughs you want.

Getting the audience to like you has nothing to do with how attractive you are or what type of voice you have. It is all about being real or at least appearing real to your audience.

As soon as you step out on stage, you need to make sure you are warm and open. Greet your audience, smile, and be friendly. Even if your on-stage persona is not so friendly, make sure you open with a warm smile so the audience knows you are glad to be there.

When you are performing your act, make sure to make eye contact with different audience members so they feel like you are talking directly to them. If you look over their heads, they will feel the disconnection and you will not engage them. The following hints will help you transform your audience into your biggest fans.

1. Make sure you speak to your audience as if they are a friend and not like you are just a big talking head on stage.
2. Show true gratitude for your audience and the attention they are giving you. Everyone likes to be praised and this will help to win them over.
3. When telling your jokes, make sure you are using inclusive pronouns such as we, us, your, and you. This puts the audience on your team.

4. Using enticing gestures will help to get your audience to fall in love with you. Smile and keep your arms open wide to welcome your audience.

5. The energy you bring to the stage will make you attractive to the audience, even if you are not physically attractive. If they are attracted to your high energy, they will love your jokes.

6. If you make mistakes during your set, make sure you own them. This will make you endeared by your audience.

No, not every audience is going to fall immediately in love with you and laugh at everything you say but using the above tips can help to win them over. The point is to make them think of you as a friend standing on stage.

How to deal with rude hecklers

Heckling is just plain rude and causes a disruption to the entire set of a stand-up comedian. Unfortunately, no comedian is immune to dealing with a loud and obnoxious audience member, no matter how good their material is.

Hecklers heckle for different reasons. Before we get started on how to deal with hecklers, let's take a quick look at why audience members might heckle. This will give you some insight into how to properly respond.

1. People heckle because they want to engage with the comedian. They actually think they are helping your act or that you expect people to participate in that manner.
2. Audience members sometimes heckle to try and embarrass the comedian. This is done as a means of showing off and is often fueled by inebriation.
3. As weird as it may sound, sometimes audience members heckle a comedian because they actually like what is being joked about. It is their inane way of endorsing the stand-up comedian.

No matter the reason, heckling happens and it can be more than a simple annoyance, especially for unseasoned comedians who are still trying to find their way on stage. Thankfully, we can look to the best comedians for advice on this subject.

While you might think you can simply ignore a heckler, some of them can be tough to ignore because they get increasingly loud and obnoxious when the comedian does not engage in their unwanted behavior. So, how do you deal with that obnoxious drunk or the one who thinks they are way funnier than you are?

- Call them on their bluff. This takes a bit of a risk but if the guy won't shut up, call him up on stage or go out to him and give him the mic. Putting him on the spot will likely get him to shut up. If it doesn't, you may have just added unexpected comedic help to your routine.

- No matter what, do not get mad. You may be fuming on the inside that someone has dared to try and ruin your act, but make sure you do not show it on the outside. Instead, make a joke of the heckling and move on.

- It is important to start off being polite to the heckler and remind them what a jerk they are being. You can say something like, "People didn't pay money to hear you whine." Often, this will stop the heckler, especially if the audience backs you up, which they likely will.

- If you plan on responding to the heckler, make sure you first repeat what the heckler said so the entire audience knows what was said and why you are responding the way you are. This engages the audience on your behalf and brings them in as backup.

- When all else fails, do not be afraid to call in security. Security guards are paid to take care of unruly guests in the club so do not worry about looking like a wimp if you need to call on them. You shouldn't have to put up with a heckler who is ruining your performance and neither should your audience, especially if they are paying to see you.

Any comedian worth their salt needs to be able to effectively deal with hecklers because they will inevitably show up when least expected. It is your job as a comedian to keep control of your audience at all times, even when a heckler is in the midst. Some comedians find it helpful to come up with a few one-liners just in case they need to throw a zinger at a disruptive heckler who is not shutting up after kindly being warned.

If the heckler gets ugly and begins to insult you, this gives you the right to insult back. Just make sure the audience understands what is going on and why you are doing what you are doing. If they have your back, you can get away with firing off insults of your own and you will likely get a laugh while doing it.

Dealing with an audience can be a rewarding and sometimes annoying experience but knowing how to deal with different situations that arise will help you to be prepared as you stand before different audiences and learn to cope with them.

As you gain practice, you will find yourself getting better and better at making audiences like you and overcoming the few who do not. In the end, let your winning personality overcome all audience obstacles that will stand in the way of you being successful at stand-up comedy.

Chapter Nine

How Do American Stand-Up Comedians Manage the Business Side of Their Career?

You've got your material all ready. You've practiced and practiced and you are even starting to gain paid gigs. If you have reached the point where you plan on making stand comedy your career or at least a money-making side job, you need to know how to properly take care of the business side of things.

From knowing how to negotiate your gig fees to deciding on hiring a manager, this chapter is devoted to helping new stand-up comedians understand how to take care of business so their talent and identity are properly protected.

Negotiating gig fees can be a daunting task

When you start getting offers to perform at clubs and shows, you are eventually going to reach the point where you are able to negotiate price. While this means you have advanced in your career, it also means you need to be ready to know how to strategically negotiate to get a fair price for your talent.

In the beginning, you are likely going to find yourself performing for free for the most part. Once it comes time for you to be able to charge for your talent, these tips will help.

Price is a subject that can be difficult to fully showcase because the amounts stand-up comedians make vary widely. A beginner comedian might start off making around $20 to $50 a night at the club while a more seasoned comedian could earn around $3,000 for a headliner weekend.

Once you become well-known in the stand-up comedy circuit, you will have more power to ask for travel expenses, accommodations, and your fee for performing. The most important thing to remember is to not ask for a star's salary when you are only a beginning comedian.

Once you have some shows under your belt and are gaining popularity, you can begin to choose an asking price. This is a bit dangerous because it could end up causing the club owner or promoter to rescind the offer.

If you begin to showboat and ask for more than your act and talent are worth, word will begin to spread quickly. You do not want to become blacklisted by all the clubs because word gets around that you are charging too much for appearances.

The following are some of the fee negotiation strategies the top comedians have used to make sure they are getting paid a fair price for their talent.

Do make sure you are confident in your approach. Know your talent and your worth but be willing to compromise based on your stand-up comedy experience.

Do make sure to seek advice and guidance from fellow stand-up comedians with more experience under their belts than you have.

Do take notes of all conversations you have with club and venue owners and promoters so you can refer to the information if needed.

Don't lie and try to tell a promoter or club owner that you are currently earning more at certain clubs or venues. This will end up backfiring because the information you provide will often be checked.

Don't be in a rush to accept the first offer you are given. Give yourself time to think about it before accepting or asking for more.

Don't apologize for the amount you are asking for. Apologizing makes you look needy and even desperate.

Don't be stubborn. Although you need to be confident, do not be stubborn and unwilling to accept fair offers.

How to keep a record of your stand-up comedy show earnings and deductions

Everyone knows they cannot get away from paying taxes so it is important you learn to keep proper records of your earnings so you can pay the IRS what they are owed. Not only will you need to keep up with your earnings, you will also need to keep up with expenses that are related to your stand-up comedy work.

In the beginning, it will be fairly easy for you to keep a simple record of all of your earnings and expenses. When you gain experience and begin making much more money in your career, you may want to make the decision to hire an accountant to help you keep your business records and file your taxes. This section is devoted to helping stand-up comedians keep careful records so they will never be concerned, should they become audited by the IRS.

A stand-up comic is considered self-employed so they will be responsible for paying taxes on any money they earn. This means careful record-keeping with an emphasis on detail. It will not help to keep a shoebox of receipts because this will end up causing confusion in your record-keeping attempts.

As a self-employed individual, you will be responsible for paying self-employment tax which is 15.3%. This is the amount of Social Security and Medicare tax that is taken out of a typical employee's check each payday.

As a self-employed stand-up comedian, you are considered an employee and an employer. The goal of filing your taxes is to reduce your tax liability by as much as possible and you will do this by keeping up with your expenses that can be deducted from your taxes. Some of the acceptable deductions include:

- Lodging
- Travel expenses
- Food

- Required equipment

If you are unsure of items you can deduct from your taxes, it is wise for you to meet with a certified accountant. Each item you deduct must be backed up with a receipt. This is why you will need to make sure you keep careful records of all of your earnings and business-related expenses.

To avoid issues with the IRS, make sure you keep your business and personal expenses entirely separate. Don't try to write off your cell phone bill if you mainly use it for personal use.

One of the easiest ways to keep a record of your earnings is a spreadsheet. This creates a chart for you to be able to easily see how much you are making and how much you are spending.

The IRS recommends self-employed individuals keep their earning and expense records for at least six years, in the event they are audited. It is wise to keep a proper filing system so you will have access to this information any time it is needed.

To keep your records for receipts, it is important you print each one out and keep them in folders that are clearly marked as food expenses, travel expenses, and lodging expenses. The better the records you keep, the less risk for developing problems when you are filing your taxes.

Should you consider hiring an agent to help with your stand-up comedy career?

Most new stand-up comedians do not need an agent or manager because they are just starting out and likely are not being paid enough. If you are serious about wanting to make stand-up comedy a career, you are going to eventually need to consider hiring someone to manage your career.

It can be difficult to rise to the top alone, no matter how talented you are. Without an agent, you will be stuck with only your own resources. Unless you know every club and venue owner in your state and surrounding ones, you are likely going to be hard-pressed to be able to book a consistent schedule.

Eventually, you are going to want to book shows in other cities across America and hiring an agent to help you get gigs will dramatically decrease the stress you experience in trying to set them up on your own.

Some of the duties an agent will perform for you include the following.

- The agent sets up all travel and lodging arrangements when you are doing a show outside of your state.

- The talent agent promotes you and works to make sure you are being booked for gigs and other events.

- Talent agents negotiate the payment amounts being offered by venue owners and promoters to ensure their client is receiving a fair price for their talent.

- These professionals will negotiate contracts on your behalf and make sure your best interests are sought in every major decision.

- The agent becomes a life coach for their client, helping them to rise as high as possible in their career and get noticed.

- Talent agents work to help their client develop the right image so they can increase their fan base and job offers.

Although you may think you can go it alone for a time, eventually, you will need to consider hiring someone to help you manage your career, especially if you want to perform live comedy on a regular basis.

Generally speaking, hiring a talent agent is going to cost you anywhere from 10% to 20% of your income as a stand-up comedian. You may want to hold off on hiring one until you start being offered more money for gigs, such as headliner opportunities.

Before hiring any manager or talent agent, make sure you carefully review the contract and have a lawyer review it as well to make sure there are no legal loopholes that could put your career or brand in jeopardy.

Chapter Ten

How to Advance Your Stand-Up Comedy Career Beyond the Small Stage

If you consider stand-up comedy to simply be a hobby, you will likely not need the advice that will be given in this chapter. If you plan on making a true career out of stand-up comedy, then you likely want to rise as high as you can, going beyond the simple stage and working towards becoming famous.

As we have said many times, rising to the top of your career is not going to be easy and you can expect many roadblocks to occur along the way. If you are willing to rise above these obstacles and keep fighting, you can have a chance to be successful in your career.

This chapter is devoted to helping rising stand-up comedy hopefuls to receive tips on how to break into television and even movies. You will also learn how to use your talents to create your own comedy specials.

It won't happen overnight, but with hard work, dedication, and these tips, you will find yourself being given a greater level of opportunity to rise above a mundane weekend career and into something that will truly get you noticed in the world of stand-up comedy.

How to break into television with top comedy shows

Most people are not willing to be stuck in a career that is not fulfilling their true potential. If you are one of these people, you are going to want to rise to the top so you can enjoy the view and the benefits.

While you may never become as famous as the likes of top comedians, this chapter will give you some valuable information that will help you pursue your dreams. As with all of the information offered in this book, you cannot simply read it and expect things to happen. It will take your hard work and dedication to make it happen so let's get started!

Television is a great way to gain a large following of fans and be offered higher-paying gigs but it is tough breaking in. The average stand-up comedian can only dream of making it to the big time but that doesn't mean you won't be able to rise above the rest and be offered television gigs.

If you want to be offered a television opportunity, your likely first pursuit will be in the form of late night television. There are now more late night television shows than ever before and many of these shows are constantly looking for up-and-coming talent to be invited to perform.

Each show has its own way of scouting out new talent. Some shows send talent scouts to live shows to view the acts of new stand-up comedians. Some ask for video or DVD submissions so they can review them and choose the ones that meet their needs.

When you are putting together a video performance of your skills, it is important you choose material that is family-friendly and suitable for late night television. While it does not have to be squeaky clean, you certainly do not want to submit a profanity-laced diatribe performance and expect to get invited.

Much like an actor auditions for television roles, you will need to prepare your "audition" DVD carefully. Your submission should fully showcase who you are as a stand-up comedian and make the producers of the show want to hire you.

Some of the biggest top comedy stars got their names out in the public and launched their careers by being invited to perform on late night television. It may take days, weeks, and months of trying but never give up on your dreams.

Talent scouts and producers look for the following when they are deciding on whether or not to invite the top comedians to perform on their show.

- Likeability
- Joke delivery
- Timing
- Uniqueness

The material you perform on late night television should not be topical because it will easily become outdated. You want material that is going to be appealing to a wide range of people. Your material should be just as funny today as it is two years from now.

The most important thing to remember is not to sell out just so you can get on television. Continue to be yourself and do what it is that makes you a unique stand-up comedian. If you stick to that, you can't go wrong, even if you never end up on the television stage.

Tips for getting stand-up comedy script roles in movies

Although television is the starting point, roles in movies can definitely help to skyrocket your career. Many stand-up comedians have been offered movie deals, including their own stand-up comedy specials that are filmed for release on DVD.

Even if you have no acting experience, it is possible for you to land a role in a comedy movie if you have what it takes to get noticed by the producers and other staff. This means you are going to have to attend auditions and stick your neck out to get noticed.

Casting directors are constantly holding casting calls that are open to just about anyone. Although some parts may have specific requirements, it never hurts to continuously seek these opportunities out.

As we spoke of in a previous chapter, hiring a manager or agent can help with casting calls. These managers are constantly seeking out new information on the latest talent opportunities and they can help their client discover opportunities they may not have been able to find on their own.

To prepare for your audition, you need to make sure you first know what the casting director is looking for. You will need to perform a short monologue that showcases your talent and your humor. As with anything regarding your career in stand-up, this means practice, practice, practice!

Make sure you do not choose a tired and overly done monologue. For the best results and to stand out as an original, consider writing your own material. That way, you can rest assured no one else will be performing the same piece before the casting director.

Realize you may fail at a casting call. Your first time may end up as a bigger failure than you can imagine. In some cases, you may be doing great at your audition but you are just not what the casting director is looking for and that's okay.

If you truly want to be serious about breaking into movies and television, you need to get a professional headshot and portfolio made. You can't simply paste a picture of yourself in your portfolio and expect this to work.

A headshot is much different from a traditional portrait because it showcases who you are as a performer and your unique attributes. In addition to your headshot, you will also need to provide the casting director with the following.

- Your resume
- Your cover letter
- A demo reel

It can be frightening auditioning for movie and television roles, especially in the beginning. If you truly want your career as a stand-up comedian to rise, you will need to launch out into the deep and get out of your comfort zone so you can be successful.

How to create your own comedy show special

You have likely watched the top comedians on their own comedy specials whether it be on DVD, HBO, or Comedy Central. There are now more opportunities for rising comedians than ever before and the market is waiting for newcomers like you.

If you are tired of waiting for gigs to open up and traveling from one venue to another, you may want to consider creating your own comedy show with the goal of having it filmed for release to the public.

There are several things you will need to keep in mind when planning your own show. These tips will help you to get started as you work towards your goal of making your own show become a reality.

- First of all, never even consider starting your own show until you have a solid set in place. This should be a tried and true set that gets laughs consistently. If you are weak in material, starting your own show will have to wait.

- Starting off small is wise when you are first creating your own comedy special show. Seek a small venue that does not have a lot of distractions and provides an intimate showcase of your talent. Smaller clubs often offer the best venues for starting off with your own show because they do not regularly get a lot of talent coming in.

- Most smaller venues do not have their own sound and lighting systems and trying to rent this equipment can end up costing you a fortune. This is not something you want when you are first trying to get a show going. Thankfully, there are smaller systems that work perfectly for more intimate venues and you should consider investing in your own system if you plan on creating shows on a regular basis.

- Make sure your show does not go over two hours and decide if you want to be the only performer or if you will invite other top comedians to perform with you. Most of the time, multi-performer acts draw in bigger crowds.

- You will likely need to hire a host to manage the night and keep everything in line, including the audience. Although you could try and manage it yourself, this will be difficult if you are performing too.

- Promoting your event begins with social media, flyers, and radio announcements. You need to get the word out to as many people who love comedy shows as possible so you can get a good crowd.

If you plan on distributing your show on DVD, you will need to hire someone to do the video work for you. This is not the time to hire your cousin Steve to perform shaky camera work. Hire a professional who has experience videoing live shows so your work will be properly showcased.

Your first comedy special show needs to be as successful as possible, without any hiccups. Don't plan on booking weekly specials at any club, bar, or other venue until you are sure your show is polished and will attract people.

Chapter Eleven

Don't Quit Your Day Job...At Least Not Yet

If you are like most people, you won't start off straight into a career of stand-up comedy alone. Most people continue to work their day job and focus on stand-up in their spare time. This chapter is focused on realistic expectations so you will not have some pie in the sky outlook that will end up being disappointing.

There are many obstacles you will face in your stand-up career and being prepared for them before you face them helps. This chapter is not meant to discourage you but, rather, to empower you to know what you are up against so you can be ready to face each obstacle head-on and jump over them.

Common obstacles for new stand-up comedians

Understanding the obstacles you might face when you launch your career in stand-up will help you to approach your career choice with an open mind, being prepared for whatever you might face. These are a few of the obstacles that may come your way as you begin pursuing a career in stand up komedi.

- You will likely struggle with what to say while you are up on stage.

- You will deal with nervousness and jitters – Even seasoned top comedians continue to get nervous.

- You will be too hard on yourself.

- You will fight for stage time in a competitive atmosphere.

- You will find it hard to be natural on stage.

- You will find it difficult to keep your material fresh at all times.

- You will find it difficult to develop a thick skin.

- You will find yourself exhausted often.

If you have read through all of the above and still feel it is worth it to pursue a career in stand-up komedi, then you are ready to get started. Launching a career in stand-up comedy is not always easy. This book would be worth nothing to you if it sugarcoated the process and made you think it was super-easy to get what you want.

Why is stand-up comedy so difficult to break into?

You know what it takes to be a stand-up comedian and what you will face as you start out on the process. Now, you need to understand why so many people find it difficult to break out into their career.

Stand-up comedy can be a brutal and unforgiving career choice and you must be the type of person who refuses to give up easily. There is now more competition than ever before and social media can make or break your career so you must be careful about every joke you tell, even if you think no one is around to see or hear it.

Just ask a few current comedians how their personal life has affected their career and you will quickly learn just how tough the stand-up comedy world is. One minute you are on top of the world and the next you are eating PB&J sandwiches for weeks.

This is why it is so important you never quit your day job until you are fully secure and have a good amount of savings. Taking the smart approach in following your dreams will help you to avoid ending up like a dried-up has-been.

As you progress in your career, you will find things never get easy. If you want a career choice that is easy, may we suggest parking cars or walking dogs? No, stand-up is not easy and it shouldn't be!

Each performance should push you to your limits and challenge you to better yourself. If you are not feeling challenged and pushed, you are caving into being mundane and this is not a place any true stand-up comedian can afford to be in.

As with any dream, you need to go all in or don't even try. Make sure you are ready to handle all of

this career, including the positives and negatives. Stand-up comedy is one of the toughest performance careers out there but it has unique benefits and thrills no other can offer.

How to speed up your success

Before we close the book, we must touch on the subject of fast-tracking your career as a stand-up comedian. Is there a way to get through the obstacles quickly without falling flat on your face? Is there a way to become one of the top comedians without going through the grind?

Although there are many schools of thought on how to become a stand-up comedian, the Internet is one way of fast-tracking. Social media affords aspiring new comedians the opportunity to get in front of an expansive audience and perform.

Every day, videos go viral for different reasons and this is how many comedians get their start. You may start off with youtube stand-up comedy and soon find yourself becoming an overnight sensation.

This does not happen to everyone but if you can create truly funny videos that appeal to a wide audience, you may be able to launch your career quickly. This is how you can get a fast start but it certainly will not keep you in the limelight if you do not have solid material and the right act.

The more content you put out there, the better the chances of you getting noticed. If you choose this route, make sure you produce stellar material that will increase the likelihood of you getting noticed.

If your videos begin to go viral and you get a large following, you can begin to make money even before you get your first stand-up comedy show. You may even end up getting invited to be on television.

While some comedy comics are able to launch their careers and gain a great Internet following, this does not happen to them all. You will need to make sure you work hard to create new content and don't be afraid to let others see your work.

This is a solid way to get your name out there while testing the waters to see if people truly like your work or if it falls flat. The Internet can become your sounding board to help you gauge your success or failure.

If you are looking for the fastest route, not necessarily the easiest, try spreading the word with the content you produce and see what happens. Even if it does not happen right away, pursuing your stand-up comedy career in this manner can help you gain confidence and try out new material without being in front of a live audience. In the end, the live stage is still your best bet for getting your name in lights, no matter how long it takes to become a success.

Conclusion

This book has now prepared you for the steps you need to take and what lies ahead as you work towards becoming a stand-up comedian. You are now armed with the information you need and it is time for you to step up to the plate and work hard.

No one can hold your hand and make it work so you've got to get prepared and be ready to be your own talent scout and promoter at first. Allow us to leave you with these parting hints to remember at all times as you pursue your career in stand-up comedy.

1. Never be afraid to go after your dreams!
2. Never stop getting on stage -do it over and over and over.
3. Never give up, even when things get tough.
4. Find your voice and master it.
5. Learn from the top comedians (from their mistakes and success).
6. Be original – Be you!
7. Always be professional.
8. Always appreciate your fans.
9. Never steal another comedian's material!
10. Don't be afraid to be successful.
11. Create your own opportunities.

12. Be persistent!
13. Listen to sound advice.
14. Be willing to adapt.
15. Understand your strengths and weaknesses.
16. Work hard even when things are tough.
17. Be honest and real at all times.
18. Don't become stuck-up if you succeed at becoming a top comedian.
19. Don't allow failures to define you.
20. Have fun!

Now, get out there, use the knowledge you have learned in this book and DO IT! You are prepared and ready with all you need to get started and now you just have to put everything you have learned into action.

Thank you for buying this book. If you would take a minute to write a review, I would very much appreciate it. It really helps me with sales and promotion.

Respectfully,
Butch Spillman

About the Author
Butch Spillman

Butch Spillman is an author with a heart for people. Born in Hollywood, California in 1946, Butch always seemed to have a dream that kept him going, even when leaving home at the tender age of 14, because he had no other choice. Life wasn't easy but Butch refused to ever give up, no matter how tough the road became.

Butch's vast career first involved him becoming a radio DJ, working the graveyard shift to pay the bills and enjoy the life experience it brought him. He would go on to work in many cities, lighting up the airways with his intoxicating personality, filled with humor and understanding.

At the age of eighteen, Butch Spillman set out on a journey to work in real estate and even acquired a General Contractor's license so he could begin building houses. He enjoyed the challenge the real estate industry brought to his life and he experienced great success in his endeavors.

Throughout his career, Butch has never stopped learning. Life taught him from an early age that he had to do for himself and keep working diligently to be successful and that is just what he did. No challenge was too great and he never accepted failures, constantly striving to better himself in all he chose to pursue.

Today, Butch is retired and although he has slowed down, he certainly has not stopped. Married to a beautiful wife, he has two grown sons and four grandchildren he loves immensely.

Throughout his life, Butch has always felt God's leading hand, guiding him on each path he has sought.

In the latest adventure of his life, Butch has set out to fulfill his lifelong dream of becoming a publisher and author. With his skills and life knowledge, he seeks to educate, enlighten, entertain, and encourage readers of all ages.

Other Kindle eBooks and Paperbacks by Butch Spillman

52 Bedtime Stories
Children's Read-Aloud Short Stories,
each with a Moral Christian Lesson

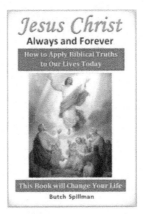

Jesus Christ, Always and Forever
How to Apply Biblical Truths
to Our Lives Today

67 Quick & Easy Italian Meals
Great Italian Recipes and Menu Ideas

1100 Fish Recipes

130 Salmon Recipes, 67 Cod Recipes, 50 Trout Recipes,
80 Halibut Recipes, 13 Red Snapper Recipes
plus over 650 more Recipes for 33 other Fish types.
Bonus Recipes include 100 Sauce Recipes,
14 Court Bouillon (Poaching Broth) Recipes,
100 Miscellaneous Fish Recipes and
27 Ways to Cook Frog Legs.

<u>Dogs have Masters,</u>
<u>Cats have Staff</u>
A Great Cat Training Guide dealing with
Cat Spraying, Cat Bed, Cat Litter, Clicker Training, etc.

<u>How to Attract Butterflies</u>
This little book shows you how fun and easy
it is to make your yard Butterfly Friendly. Learn
how to get their attention with bright colored plants,
sunny areas, wind protection, butterfly spas, and more...